MACARONI AND CHEESE: AN OUT-OF-THE-BOX STORY

THE DISH ON THE DISH: A HISTORY OF YOUR FAVORITE FOODS

JULIE KNUTSON

CHERRY LAKE PRESS

Published in the United States of America by Cherry Lake Publishing Group
Ann Arbor, Michigan
www.cherrylakepublishing.com

Reading Adviser: Reading Adviser: Beth Walker Gambro, MS, Ed., Reading Consultant, Yorkville, IL
Photo Credits: © Jennifer White Maxwell/Shutterstock.com, cover, 1; © pamela_d_mcadams/iStock.com, 5; © Ezume Images/Shutterstock.com, 6; © vitals/Shutterstock.com, 8; © OnlyFOOD/Shutterstock.com, 9; © Maxwell Photography/Shutterstock.com, 10; © Volkova/Shutterstock.com, 13; © MaraZe/Shutterstock.com, 14; © Ozgur Coskun/Shutterstock.com, 16; © Jiri Hera/Shutterstock.com, 17; © Steve Cukrov/Shutterstock.com, 18; © YesPhotographers/Shutterstock.com, 21; © Ika Rahma H/Shutterstock.com, 23; © Lukas Gojda/Shutterstock.com, 24; © gowithstock/Shutterstock.com, 27; © Brendan Lekan/Shutterstock.com, 28

Cherry Lake Press is an imprint of Cherry Lake Publishing Group.

Library of Congress Cataloging-in-Publication Data

Names: Knutson, Julie, author.
Title: Macaroni and cheese : an out-of-the-box story / Julie Knutson.
Description: Ann Arbor, Michigan : Cherry Lake Publishing, [2022] | Series: The dish on the dish: a history of your favorite foods | Includes index. | Audience: Grades 4-6
Identifiers: LCCN 2021006136 (print) | LCCN 2021006137 (ebook) | ISBN 9781534187320 (hardcover) | ISBN 9781534188723 (paperback) | ISBN 9781534190122 (pdf) | ISBN 9781534191525 (ebook)
Subjects: LCSH: Cooking (Pasta) | Cooking (Cheese) | Casserole cooking. | LCGFT: Cookbooks.
Classification: LCC TX809.M17 K58 2021 (print) | LCC TX809.M17 (ebook) | DDC 641.82/2–dc23
LC record available at https://lccn.loc.gov/2021006136
LC ebook record available at https://lccn.loc.gov/2021006137

Cherry Lake Publishing Group would like to acknowledge the work of the Partnership for 21st Century Learning, a Network of Battelle for Kids. Please visit http://www.battelleforkids.org/networks/p21 for more information.

Printed in the United States of America
Corporate Graphics

ABOUT THE AUTHOR

Julie Knutson is an author who lives in northern Illinois with her husband, son, and border collie. She prefers her pancakes with Nutella and bananas, her pizza "Detroit-style," and her mac 'n' cheese with little green peas.

TABLE OF CONTENTS

First Plating

At its core, it's a simple recipe of four ingredients: butter, cheese, milk, and noodles. But for so many people, it's much, *much* more than that. It's pure comfort—the food equivalent of a hug, a high five, or a family holiday—served on a plate or in a bowl. Whether you prefer it with a spoon, a fork, or a spork, it's the oozy, warming goodness that is . . . MACARONI AND CHEESE.

Today, there are endless varieties. You can rip open a box of noodles and a packet of cheese to fix yourself a quick out-of-the box meal. Or you can go to a gourmet restaurant like Jus' Mac in Houston, Texas, and order a version with **bulgogi** and kimchi slaw. Its popularity and openness to interpretation begs a key question: Where did this dish come from? Who thought it up?

Kraft® uses their own unique noodles in their macaroni and cheese.

Macaroni and cheese can be mixed with veggies like broccoli.

And how did it get to be a food that nearly everyone has tried at some point?

First, let's break the dish down into its namesake parts: macaroni *and* cheese. Macaroni is a type of noodle, a food form with a long history that twists across multiple continents. Archaeological and written evidence shows that people have eaten noodles—made by mixing grains with water, forming them into a shape, and cooking them—for thousands of years. In 2005, archaeologists in northwest China found a perfectly preserved 4,000-year-old bowl of noodles made of **millet**. It was buried in the rubble of a prehistoric earthquake! Noodles can be made fresh and eaten immediately, or they can be dried and preserved for later use.

Cheese also has a lengthy history. Around 10,000 years ago, the world's first cheesemakers figured out how to make **perishable** dairy products last longer. The oldest surviving evidence of cheese dates to 3,200 years ago. In the tomb of an ancient Egyptian official, archaeologists found a broken jar containing a solid white mass. Analysis showed this cheese was made of milk from goats and sheep.

"Yankee Doodle" . . . It's a common tune hummed by kid campers and field-trippers alike. But what does it mean to stick a feather in one's hat and "call it macaroni"? In England in the mid-1700s, the term "macaroni" described super-hip youth who sported big wigs and tight jackets. During the American Revolution, it's believed it was originally used as an insult by the British against the American colonists, for whom fashion-forward meant . . . putting a feather in your cap and calling it cutting-edge. Or "macaroni."

Macaroni noodles come in all sorts of shapes, including shells and bow ties!

While noodles and cheese both have prehistoric origins, they don't seem to have been formally introduced to each other until the Middle Ages. A royal Italian cookbook from the 13th century describes square pasta covered with grated cheese. It might have been an early version of lasagna! The dish migrated to other European courts, appearing in an English cookbook from 1390. In this version, butter was added to the pasta and grated cheese. In the Swiss Alps, yet another variation appeared. In this harsh mountain climate, a rich and nourishing meal made of noodles, cheese, butter, cream, potatoes, and onions sustained many a herder.

Pasta dough is made by combining eggs with flour and salt.

Macaroni and cheese is also called mac 'n' cheese.

In the 18th century, President Thomas Jefferson ate macaroni and cheese in Europe. During this time, mac 'n' cheese was gaining popularity in England and France. For Jefferson, it was love at first bite. The future president went so far as to smuggle an Italian pasta-making machine across the Atlantic to his Virginia estate, Monticello. While Jefferson didn't "invent" mac 'n' cheese and was unlikely the first person to bring it to the United States—macaroni pudding was a common dish at New England church suppers—he did help popularize it. Macaroni and cheese was so treasured in

Jefferson's recipe box that it was even served at an 1802 White House dinner. Massachusetts Congressional Representative Manasseh Cutler was underwhelmed by this "macaroni pie," mistaking the noodles for potatoes. He further noted that the dish "tasted very strong, and not agreeable." Cutler would have a hard time believing that in the century to follow, it would become one of the nation's most **iconic** foods.

James Hemings (1765–1801)

Thomas Jefferson often gets credit for introducing macaroni and cheese to America. But the dish probably wouldn't have been served in the newly minted United States without chef James Hemings. Jefferson didn't prepare his own food. His meals were made by enslaved workers, including Hemings.

While serving as Minister to the French court, Jefferson brought Hemings with him to France. There, Hemings trained as a chef for 3 years—the first African American to do so. When Hemings asked Jefferson for his freedom in the 1790s, Jefferson granted it on two conditions. First, he had to train the other members of the household kitchen staff to cook his dishes. Second, all of his recipes had to be recorded. After Hemings left Jefferson's home, he worked in Philadelphia, Pennslyvania, and Baltimore, Maryland. He possibly also worked in Europe. He died in 1801.

CHAPTER 2

Migrations

With expensive ingredients and presidential fans, mac 'n' cheese was an **elite** dish in the first part of the 19th century. Cookbooks like *The Virginia House-Wife*, published in 1824 by Mary Randolph—a relative of Thomas Jefferson—brought attention to this pairing of carbs and cheese. With printed recipes available, it became a **staple** of weekend and holiday meals in the southern United States.

Around the mid-1800s, several changes paved the way toward mac 'n' cheese for all. The **Industrial Revolution** allowed pasta and cheese to be mass-produced. In 1848, the first U.S. pasta factory

In factories, macaroni noodles are sorted on conveyor belts.

Whole milk makes for a creamy addition to macaroni and cheese.

opened in Brooklyn, New York. The factory was literally horse-powered. According to the *Chicago Tribune,* its machinery ran on **equine** energy. The machine-made noodles were then air-dried on the factory's roof. In 1851, America's first cheese factory opened in Rome, New York. With this, cheese went from being a farm to a factory product.

By the early 20th century, a popular **Creole** cookbook noted that mac 'n' cheese was widely eaten in New Orleans, Louisiana. The dish also became a staple of African American celebrations

Milk is white . . . so why is cheese sometimes orange? The color of cheese results from the diet of the cow that produced the milk used to make it. Historically, yellowish cheeses—produced with milk from grass-fed heifers—fetched higher prices. Sneaky cheesemakers added dyes to white cheeses so that they could charge more for them.

Macaroni can be baked in many different vessels.

and special occasions. Well-known Black chef Rufus Estes featured it in his 1911 cookbook, *Good Things to Eat, As Suggested by Rufus.* In this recipe, Estes advised layering cheese and noodles in a pudding dish for the perfect bake. During the **Great Migration**, many African Americans from the Deep South were drawn to northern industrial cities by the promise of better work, housing, and education. Food traditions, like mac 'n' cheese, came with them.

There are many cheeses that can make a good macaroni.

Kraft® released their single serve cups in 2006.

While some continued to cook mac 'n' cheese from scratch, it became a cheap, fast food for others in the 1930s. In 1937, at the height of the **Great Depression**, Kraft® introduced its "meal for four in nine minutes." At just 19 cents a box, this inexpensive source of protein appealed to families struggling to make ends meet. In its first year, the product sold a whopping 8 million boxes! Its popularity endured during World War II as **rationing** of meat and dairy went into effect. Today, it's still a hit with grocery shoppers. A million of these blue boxes are sold every day.

While the world consumes a lot of boxed mac 'n' cheese, it's not the globe's most popular pantry staple. That honor belongs to instant ramen noodles, which were invented in Japan in 1958. Worldwide, approximately 100 billion servings of instant noodles are slurped up each year.

CHAPTER 3

Evolution and Wild Variations

Today, entire restaurants devoted to mac 'n' cheese exist in Florida, California, and New York. Macaroni and cheese fans can attend annual festivals in Minnesota, California, and New Mexico. If dairy isn't your thing, you can try a vegan version made by companies like Mac & Yease® or Annie's® Organic. And it's not just an American thing. Noodles and cheese are combined with different results in different corners of the world. Let's take a tour of the globe to see what you can get in Canada, the Caribbean, and beyond.

There's no limit to the amount of cheese you can add to your macaroni.

Let's begin in Germany. On a cold and snowy night, treat yourself to a hearty plate of käsespätzle. These chewy, twisty egg noodles covered in Jarlsberg cheese reflect the dish's roots in the Swiss Alps.

Travel even further north to Finland, where you can try out makaronilaatikko. This **casserole** adds ground beef and onion to the traditional mix of noodles and creamy cheese. As in Canada, it's traditionally topped with an unexpected **condiment** . . .

That's right, ketchup. Each year, Canada out-consumes its neighbor to the south in mac 'n' cheese, taking the title for the "Kraftiest" nation. Sometimes simply called the "Kraft® Dinner"—or KD for short—it's been mentioned in songs. Former Prime Minister Paul Martin said it's his favorite meal.

In October 2020, rapper and actor Drake shocked the food world and his fans alike. At his 34th birthday party, he served a beloved dish of his native Canada—macaroni and cheese—with raisins, sun-dried tomatoes, capers, and parsley. What do you think? Would you try Drake's take on the classic?

When baked in a casserole dish, macaroni and cheese can get a delicious crispy top.

Cheddar remains one of the most common cheeses in macaroni.

If you're looking for a warmer climate, head to Barbados. A crustless dish, macaroni pie is sometimes served cold. Crushed black pepper, curry powder, and hot sauce frequently up the dish's spice level. It's often served with fish, chicken, pork, or stew.

Greece's mild climate offers yet another version of the dish. Pastitsio is often compared to lasagna. A layer of ground meat is wedged between a base of penne noodles and a blanket of oozy béchamel sauce.

Last stop? Indonesia. Mac 'n' cheese was introduced to the South Pacific nation by Dutch colonists. Macaroni schotel reinvents the traditional dish with local flavors and ingredients. Beyond the base of milk, cheese, butter, and noodles, expect additions like smoked beef, sausage, tuna, eggs, onion, mushrooms, and potatoes.

Did you know that there are "pasta architects"? Perhaps the most famous of these designers is Guillermo Haro, who draws up cartoony shapes for Kraft®. In 2013, Smithsonian *magazine reported that Haro has designed more than 2,000 pasta shapes, with 280 of those finding a life on the shelf!*

CHAPTER 4

Make Your Own!

Believe it or not, you can make mac 'n' cheese in the microwave. Create this super-fast and easy version of the dish for your family. You can keep it classic or add your own twist by topping it with avocado, bacon bits, or spinach. The options are endless!

INGREDIENTS:

- ½ cup (128 grams) elbow macaroni
- ½ cup (120 milliliters) water
- ¼ cup (32 g) shredded cheddar cheese
- A splash of milk
- Salt
- Pepper

Bacon is a salty treat to add to your macaroni and cheese.

DIRECTIONS:

1. Pour the pasta and water into a microwave safe cup or bowl. Add a pinch of salt.
2. Microwave for 2 to 3 minutes to cook the pasta.
3. Add milk, cheese, and pepper to taste. Stir!
4. Return to the microwave for 30 more seconds.
5. Let cool. Dive in!

Macaroni and cheese is considered a comfort food.

10 Delightfully Cheesy Facts

- Did you know the United States has a National Macaroni and Cheese Day? This carb-lovers holiday falls on July 14.
- According to *Guinness World Records,* the largest macaroni and cheese ever made weighed 2,469 pounds (1,120 kilograms). The record was set in New Orleans, Louisiana, on September 23, 2010.
- Canadians are major consumers of Kraft® macaroni and cheese, buying 12 percent of the world's total each year. A 2019 survey showed that 63 percent of Canadians have a box of the blue stuff in their pantries.
- Kraft® sells 1 million boxes of macaroni and cheese per day!
- Cheddar makes up almost 90 percent of cheese sold in the United States.
- In the United States alone, Kraft® sells 350 million boxes of macaroni and cheese each year. Canadians consume about 94 million boxes in the same period.
- For more than 200 years, seeds from the annatto tree have been used to give processed cheddars their bright orange color.
- In August 2020, Kraft® announced a limited-edition product, a macaroni and cheese "Breakfast Box." Alongside its regular box of macaroni, it also includes a mug, a placement for coloring, and a magnet with breakfast topping ideas.
- According to the British Broadcasting Corporation, in any given 12 week period, approximately half of all children in the United States will eat mac 'n' cheese at least once.
- A 2007 survey by the James Beard Foundation placed mac 'n' cheese as the fourth most iconic American food, after hamburgers, barbecue, and fried chicken.

Timeline

1390 In England, a cookbook titled *The Forme of Cury*, meaning *Method of Cooking*, Includes a recipe for a precursor to mac 'n' cheese as we know it.

1802 President Thomas Jefferson serves macaroni pie to guests at the White House.

1824 Mary Randolph's mac 'n' cheese recipe appears in *The Virginia House-Wife* cookbook.

1851 The first cheese factory in the United States opens in Rome, New York.

1911 Noted African American chef Rufus Estes includes a macaroni and cheese recipe in his cookbook, *Good Things to Eat, As Suggested by Rufus*.

1937 Kraft® begins selling boxed macaroni and cheese, marketing it as a complete meal in a box.

1943 Mac 'n' cheese sales soar in the United States during World War II rationing of meat and dairy.

1993 Crayola® names a crayon color "Macaroni and Cheese" in a nod to the beloved dish.

2010 The largest mac 'n' cheese ever made is assembled in New Orleans, Louisiana.

2016 Kraft® removes artificial coloring from its products.

Further Reading

BOOKS

Leaf, Christina. *Macaroni & Cheese.* Minneapolis, MN: Bellwether Media, 2020.

Sullivan, Jaclyn. *What's in Your Macaroni and Cheese?* New York, NY: PowerKids Press, 2012.

WEBSITES

Chicago Tribune—Macaroni & Cheese: A Deliciously American Timeline
www.chicagotribune.com/dining/ct-macaroni-and-cheese-timeline-gallery-0317-photogallery.html
Check out this timeline of macaroni and cheese in America.

Wonderopolis—Why Is Cheddar Cheese Orange?
www.wonderopolis.org/wonder/why-is-cheddar-cheese-orange
Check out this website to learn more about macaroni and cheese.

GLOSSARY

bulgogi (BOOL-goh-gee) thinly sliced Korean meat

casserole (KASS-uh-role) a side dish cooked slowly in an oven

condiment (KAHN-duh-muhnt) a substance that adds flavor to food, like ketchup

Creole (KREE-ohl) a mix of European and African cultural influences

elite (i-LEET) someone or something considered to have power and influence

equine (EE-kwine) related to horses

Great Depression (GRAYT di-PRESH-uhn) the period of global economic decline that lasted from 1929 until 1939

Great Migration (GRAYT mye-GRAY-shuhn) the mass migration of African Americans from the rural South to industrial northern cities

iconic (eye-KON-ik) famous and widely recognized

Industrial Revolution (in-DUHSS-tree-uhl rev-uh-LOO-shuhn) the large social and economic shift toward machine and factory-produced goods

millet (MIH-luht) ancient grain used to make some types of flour

perishable (PER-ih-shuh-buhl) food product that spoils

rationing (RASH-uhn-ING) the act of allowing each person only a fixed amount of something, especially when resources need to be conserved

staple (STAY-puhl) a core element of a diet

INDEX